CW01025079

Forthcoming title by June Kidd:

"The Pruning of the Vine"

Previous titles:

"Unshriven"

"Jesus, D.I.Y and You The Human Magnet"

See website for details of events and talks:
www.junekidd.com

THE AUTHOR

June left the pace and excitement of working in and around New York to be married in New Orleans, before moving with her husband, a physician, to Saudi Arabia.

There she spent the next ten years, savouring the exotic Middle Eastern culture, living, working and enjoying the company of people from all over the world and also co-founding the first school for children with Down's Syndrome.

She also travelled extensively to Europe, China, Australia, America and the Caribbean.

It was during a home visit to England that June began her intensive study of 'Imagination, meditation and mental discipline,' eventually becoming an advanced graduate of The Silva Method.

The decision to take this course was to transform and enhance her life, particularly as a writer, freeing her from a lifelong handicap with dyslexia, learning to spell virtually overnight at the age of 40, and developing a heightened 'Spiritual Sensitivity,' that enabled her to write *Unshriven*, her first book.

ACKNOWLEDGEMENTS

My love and thanks to my dear husband Roland, for his wisdom, constant support and proof-reading, and to my dear family for their never failing encouragement.

To Neil Wellington for his technical support and for always answering SOS calls.

To Felix Morris-Duffin for his website support and formatting of this book.

Finally, to the Silva Method, the foundation of my philosophy.

CONTENTS

JESUS, D.I.Y AND YOU
THE HUMAN MAGNET

This book is dedicated to Jose Silva, founder
of The Silva Method

JUNE KIDD

JESUS

THE SECOND COMING

Forgive me but I am constantly amazed by the optimism of people who, doing nothing to take themselves out of their comfort zone, are sitting back and waiting for **"THE SECOND COMING"**, a time when another **"Saviour"** will appear on earth and, with a few well chosen words (or a wave of a magic wand) explain (again) where we have been going wrong and make the bad guys (always other people) toe the line.

(If you are one of those people who adamantly believe that only a 'Second Coming', can save the world, well you might be right - but there is nothing in the teaching of Jesus that says you should wait until then, to put his amazing teachings into daily practice.)

A second coming? Yes - but get used to this idea:

YOU ARE IT!

(This not a new idea: The Hopi Indians prophesy says:
"We *are the ones we have been waiting for.")*

Jesus voiced his hopes and <u>expectations</u>, when he said: "Whatever I do, you can do, and more." So you have to wake up to the <u>possibility</u> that no Saviour is going to come back here to be a dumping ground for society's responsibilities. Those days have gone but to believe that a loving intelligent God would leave man in bondage, would be to dishonor the Creator we call God.
There is a way out and Jesus said: "Whatever I do, you can do, and more."

How? Well, if you study what he actually said, if you examine the words, you will find that he is repeatedly telling you <u>how!</u> And it is so simple!

The key - the first thing to understand, is that there is one amazingly simple powerful universal law that governs everything, that is the law of **Like attracting Like**. The ignorance of this law can make or break you and the dismissal of it can see opportunities pass just out of reach, sapping your confidence, your hopes and your dreams until you finally let go and turn away, disillusioned and accepting that you are not the master of your fate.

'LIKE ATTRACTING LIKE' IS A UNIVERSAL LAW AND NOTHING IS EXEMPT FROM IT

(In science it is called the Law of Entrainment, as in Space, when smaller less dynamic objects are swept into the train of the faster moving, more energized force; for example Hayley's comet.)

The wisest teachers and the most successful and productive people who have ever lived, understood how it works, and recognized our ability to use the power of our minds to attract to us what we want - and what we don't want! From Jesus to Plato, Shakespeare to Sir Francis Bacon, Victor Hugo to Beethoven, from Goethe to Sir Isaac Newton, William Blake to Madam Blavatsky (Founder of the Theosophical Society) Earnest Holmes (founder of Science of Mind) and Jose Silva, (founder of The Silva Method, and the source of my personal development.)

(See www.junekidd.com) All these people sent out variations of this same message, one that is central to the teachings of Jesus, one that recurs throughout the bible.

For example - in the book of Job:

Job. 3:25 states: "For what I fear comes upon me, and what I dread befalls me."
Mark 11:2 "What things so-ever ye desire, when ye pray, believe that ye have them and ye shall have them."
Mathew 21:22 "Whatsoever ye ask in prayer, believing, ye shall receive."
Mark 11:24 *"What things soever ye desire, when ye pray, believe ye receive them*
And ye shall have them"

So take charge of your thinking and take charge of your life. Focus on what you want.

If you want an example of what can be achieved by the focusing of the mind, study modern day entrepreneurs; their seemingly boundless energy, vitality and optimism influence and excite us to aim higher and do more with our time here. How do they achieve this powerful position? They achieve so much because they believe in themselves and believe in their ability to make things work for them; their focus is on what they want to happen. They don't spend time and energy dwelling on doubts because they know that minute-by-minute, they are creating the quality of their own reality; the Universe responds to power of thought - good, bad or indifferent. They are never bored. Boredom brings weariness to the body and spirit but enthusiasm is a high revving energy that thrives on challenge. Both are directly influenced by attitude.

They are, and we are, <u>magnets</u>, using the greatest power in the universe, the power of <u>thought</u>, to attract to us what we are focusing on, even if it is failure or mediocrity or self-destruction. You do this mostly without realising it – and that is scary! Until you snap out of this dream-like 'accepting *whatever fate throws your way' mentality, and give thought to how you might be influencing 'the system,' your life will continue to be a very hit and miss affair. This most powerful force in the Universe responds to what we focus on, be it consciously or unconsciously, and assuming it is what we want more of, lovingly and without judgment, delivers more of the same. So if you are content to drift through life, you will get whatever drifts your way.*

Some say that <u>if another Saviour came now</u>, (and first ask yourself, who would risk it, after the send-off we gave Jesus?) one half of the world's population would want to kill him, and at best, the rest would dismiss him as a fake or a hologram!

Alternatively, <u>if another Saviour came now</u>, there would be an outcry from fundamentalist religious groups that this crank is a charlatan from the other-side: Muslim/Christian/Catholic/Buddhist; (you name it) and "How dare <u>they</u> assume that the <u>real</u> Saviour would come to them, when in fact WE are the only true religion because we worship God in this (or that) way?" *And what if it were a woman? (Music to the Hitchcock film, Psycho!)*

<u>If another Saviour came now</u>, few would take notice: "Oh yes, eternal life? I'll think about that later, what's for now?' We are all too busy anticipating the next problem such as the people next door, a work colleague, more tax, drugs, new tyres for the car etc, to give ourselves time to think. Make your own list. It's very enlightening. It will show the direction of your focus of attention; negative, positive or just stuck in the middle!).

I AM THE WAY, THE TRUTH AND THE LIGHT

"**I am the way**." His knew the way we could escape from the bondage of this nightmare world we have created for ourselves.

"**I am the truth.**" He was not part of the Illusion we call Reality.

"**I am the Light.**" Light means Enlightenment; understanding and unlocking the secret to our own power. He was shining the light on the path to freedom. In saying, **"Do this in my name."** I humbly suggest he wasn't saying literally, in the name of **Jesus**. He was saying do this in the name of what I stand for.

This world is governed from its very roots by fear in all of its various forms. If the Universe keeps receiving mental pictures that always involve enemy, it assumes that what we are focusing on, we want more of;

conflict and more things to be afraid of. It then delivers, without judgment, more of the same. Jesus came to explain this, how, without our realising it, we are creating our own fate. He came here to educate us, tell us how the systems work, not to give us another figurehead to be subservient to.

(He did not mean to do these things in the actual name of Jesus. Jesus was and still is a common name in the Middle and Far East and in Latin America).

NATIONAL GALLERY, LONDON.

There is a huge painting in the National Gallery, London, by the 17th century artist, Gerrit van Honthorst, called:

Christ before the High Priest.

Christ, his hands bound, stands before the High Priest. A small table between them, a single lighted candle, the elderly, sour looking priest, finger pointing, is quoting from a Holy Book, and telling Jesus that only he, as the High Priest, knows how to interpret God's words.

Jesus, his task almost at an end, is deeply saddened but resigned – yet it is the way the artist has portrayed the expression in the eyes of Jesus that takes the breath away. If one picture is worth 1,000 words, then this says all that Jesus would have been thinking:

"I desired to give you back the greatest of gifts, your freedom, yet you cling to the mean and the sordid and preach fear."

The expression on His face is one of worldly weariness; accepting and no longer involved in the struggle of words. He hopes that he has been able to do enough to help educate the world out of its ignorance. His greatest challenge is soon to come and He knows it, yet there is no conflict - He is at peace. His final act of love to this stricken world is yet to come; nailed to the cross, He will not retract his message; we are not powerless and we are not alone.

One enormous and final challenge then he will soon be in his own loving, sane, spiritually evolved dimension; the true Reality.

(For this planet is no example of rational thinking and what we accept as 'reality' is in fact a fear-driven illusion, one that is sending shock waves down the backbone of the rest of the Universe)

Jesus said of his miracles: **<u>"This you can do, and more,"</u>** and so now comes the decision; you either have to accept that he knew what we were capable of (and so be faced with the challenge and responsibility of putting his words into practice) or admit to yourself that you are not motivated to do anything to improve this world crisis.) You could of course use the 'cop-out clause' and say that he didn't really know the challenges of living in modern times on this mentally polluted planet.

Uncomfortable, isn't it?

THIS IS NOT A RELIGIOUS BOOK

When I use the name, God, I would like to explain that for my part, I see God as the Divine Force, a collective energy of Pure Wisdom and Pure Love. This entity allows us free will so that we will grow in wisdom, through experience; like a wise loving parent, who knows that the child has to go out into the world and learn, often by mistakes.

For the sake of clarity and to stop some of you more sensitive or ridged souls being offended, please understand that in this book, when I speak of God, or the God Energy or Oneness, when I speak of Jesus as a teacher or a philosopher, when I say Guardian Angel of the Universal Mind, or Saviour or Devine consciousness or Supreme Creator, it means what <u>YOU</u> want it to mean. It is your idea of a figurehead, so no one need be offended. There is no offence intended. O.K?

In quoting from people throughout history who knew of and used this Law of Like Attracting Like/The Law of Attraction, we cannot but re-examine the simple teachings of Jesus. Central to all of his talks and parables, Jesus taught the <u>power</u> of love and forgiveness and <u>how</u> 'The Law' (always reacting whether we know it or not) is constantly at work. The following story is a perfect example.

JESUS & THE POWER OF
ATTRACTION

Jesus was walking through a crowd, people pulling and tugging at his clothes, imploring him to heal them and learn for them and change their lives with yet another miracle: A woman, kneeling down, quietly reached out to touch his garment, believing absolutely that by doing so, she would be healed. Amid all that noise and pushing and shoving and touching, Jesus suddenly stopped, turned and said: "Who has touched me?"

(Think of that for a moment. Think of a pop star in a crowd of fans. Would you notice if one person touched your coat?) But Jesus notices; felt her pure energy, her power of attraction. Without her understanding it, the energy, the total belief with which she had touched his cloak, had been of the Divine Power, the Universal Mind, and he said:

"Woman, <u>thy faith</u> has made thee whole." (And he wasn't referring to any hero worship or her faith in him. She

16

had faith in his words, in his philosophy. It made total sense to her and she acted upon it and got her reward.

Inside his head he must have been yelling, "She got it! By Heaven, she's got it! She has understood and believed in her own ability. She is using her power of attraction to get what she wants; self-healing! Halleluiah, someone truly understands; a breakthrough, at last!" In all that mad crowd, that woman knew how slim her chances were of actually getting a 'one to one' with Jesus but she had her own unbending belief and that was the greatest gift she could give to the world and to this good man; one who suffered horrendous torture rather take away our first glimpse of the truth…

QUOTES FROM THE BIBLE

"Cast your bread upon the waters and it will return tenfold."

Using bread as a symbol, it can refer to your wealth or even your understanding of the Law of Return. (Like attracts like.)

Bible quotes: "It is harder for a rich man to get into the Kingdom of God than for a camel to get through the eye of a needle."

This similarly must have made people laugh – and pay attention! But this does not mean that having money is bad. Money is very good if you do a lot of good with it. If you are making money and spreading it around (sowing the seeds, making things grow), utterly confident that more will come in to cover your needs, then you will keep yourself in the flow of bounty.

If however (like a miser) you hang on to your wealth, fearful that you will not have enough, then you will never *feel* you have enough and you will never ever feel free to enjoy it.

"Give no man evil for evil." Flashing back hate for hate or anger for anger is like the flashing of electricity between two metal poles; it never stops, and a fixation on suspicion or mistrust, (just like in a family vendetta) can take over a whole life and destroy a family.

You may have heard the saying: "*To know all is to forgive all*," and you might find that very hard to believe. However, anger, hate, suspicion, vindictiveness, bullying, all stem from one source, for the perpetrator has a vulnerability, a fear of lack; lack of love, reputation, money, home, job, fear that if I don't hurt him he will hurt me. All these things can initiate fear. There is always a reason...

A strong mind can help make anything better. Think of Jesus nailed to the cross. With all the good he had done in this world, this was his reward and surely a time when he could have, quite understandably, rained mayhem on those torturing him. But in doing so he would have made a mockery, and a nonsense of his message of love and instruction to 'Give no man evil for evil'. This was the ultimate test of love and yet, hanging there he still called out; "Father, forgive them for they know not what they do." (They don't know that they are operating the Law of Attraction/like attracting like). Even in those dire hours, he did not want them to face suffering as he had. What courage! What dedication to his task on Earth. He was willing for thei powerful energy of their hate to be spent, heaped on his shoulders and so become neutralized. So, no matter what the circumstances, as long as you have conviction and a strong mind, you can keep your integrity and cope with the most undermining situations and make any situation more bearable, as did Jesus. The power really is all in the mind.

A CHANGING WORLD

Throughout the world, the old ways are dying. Don't mourn the change, remembering only the good times, cosseted and viewed through the pink tinted glasses of nostalgia. Sadly, the old ways have brought us and this planet to its knees. If you are suspicious of the New Age, this New Way of thinking, well just look around you and see where the Old Way of thinking has got us!

"It's nothing to do with me." I hear you distance yourself from the chaotic state we are in. "I'm one of the good guys. I've done nothing." No? Well, all that is required for evil to succeed is for good men to do nothing!

We're all guilty of "Doing those things we ought not to have done and leaving undone those things we ought to have done…" and that includes you.

And don't spend time worrying about Hell and the Devil. There is nothing, absolutely nothing, that any devil could do to us which we have not done, or are still doing to each other.

So why not work to a structure that will help your improved life by keeping this guideline, set out by Don Miguel Ruiz, in his book "The Four Agreements"

Don Miguel has his own examples of these four agreements, just inside the cover of his book, but here I give mine.

1) Be impeccable with your words.

Don't spread gossip and think on this: It might be true but perhaps it's kinder not to say so: Great minds discuss ideas; average minds discuss events; small minds discuss other people.

(SHAKESPEARE was saying this when he wrote):

Good name in man and woman, dear my lord.

Is the immediate jewel of their souls.
Who steals my purse steals trash; 'tis
something, nothing;
'Twas mine, 'tis his, and has been slave to
thousands;
But he that filches from me my good name
Robs me of that which not enriches him,
And makes me poor indeed.
Othello Act 3, scene 3, 155–161

2) Don't take anything personally.

(If someone is abrupt, they may be stressed out from a hell of a day, so they won't respond sympathetically to the first person who gets 'in line,' you!

Rarely is it directly because of you. They are simply reacting to what is happening in their lives. So don't take it personally. Relax, and wait.

Remember, there is always a reason…

3) Don't make assumptions.

(Jumping to conclusions or making assumptions is a reflex action and one that causes so much unhappiness and misunderstanding. The next time you think you've been slighted, don't react in the old way but remind yourself of this 'agreement' and wait; let the earth turn a few times.

Most misunderstandings clear themselves, given time.

4) Always do your best.

Under all circumstances, simply do your best. No one can do more.

Remember to say, thank you, when you make a request to the Universe and also when it is delivered; keep that two way connection strong because like

Google, the Universal Mind, is always updating - and it's good to be on the first page!

TRY CHANGING YOUR ATTITUDE

From the memorable, beautifully written and heart lifting autobiography of William Blatty (Author of The Exorcist) 'I'LL TELL THEM I REMEMBER YOU.'
I trust that Peter will not mind my using his fine example.

Peter's mother was what could be described as a 'power house,' an immigrant from Lebanon who sailed with her husband and children to the U.S.A. on a cattle boat. Very poor and later without a husband, she somehow supported her family until finally, only Peter (still a small boy) was left at home. A gleaming new grocery store had just opened nearby on Third Avenue, close to Thirty-fifth Street. Peter and his mama, on their way home after a wearisome day dodging in and out of crowds, trying to sell Mrs. Blatty's home-made quince jam, were just in time to buy basic milk and potatoes as the store closed up for the night.
Peter carried the bag: 'It was late and I was tired and the bag seemed heavy.' When we got home,

Mama opened the bag and gasped! It was filled with the grocery's income for the day. The assistant, obviously very tired too, had apparently mixed the bag up as they were both on the counter and of equal size. The grocery people didn't know us from a mango; it was the first time we had been there.

My Mother stared at the money for a while and then slowly and mutely, she closed up the bag and instructed me to take it back to the store.

'I picked it up again and this time it felt light. And for once I felt the thrill of great power unused, which a man needs to feel only once in his lifetime to sense he is more cousin to the Angels than the apes…'

We all have the power to change the daily reality we live.
It really is an attitude of mind.

WE ARE ALL TEACHERS

Jesus passionately wanted us to believe in our own ability to use and relay the message of self-empowerment, not by trying to 'convert' anyone to your way of thinking, but by your confident, successful, happy example. You will know that what you are doing is the right thing, by the grace and ease with which your life flows, and that is all the example needed. No need to preach. Just 'live the life.'

Above all, Jesus was a practical man who came here to do a practical job as an educator. He didn't come to this planet with a brief to dish up happy days to cheer us or miracles to entertain us or words to reassure us that he would take care of all our problems, or that we need do nothing but pay homage! (That's like a child relying on dear old dad. That's fine for a child but not when it turns 35! It's D.I.Y. time now!)

28

Jesus had no ego, he didn't want our subservience. He didn't go through Hell and back again to get a fan club or start a new religion, or be 'mystified' out of our reach. Saying that is just a clever way of ditching your responsibilities and having an excuse to do nothing that requires you to come out of your comfort zone. You're not fooling anyone, especially yourself.

Christianity mean love and kindness and should be a way of life. The Church is where you attend for instruction, collective prayer (always very powerful) and counseling. If that's where you find the most support, then that's the way for you to go - but don't let the instruction you hear from those highly educated and dedicated clergy end on Sunday! Your 'living the ideal' is their reward.

Having said that, these people have to earn a living and keep the buildings in good repair. That costs money. In the Bible it says: 'The labourer (in this case the clergy) is worthy of his hire.' So, if you use the church for any reason, you should contribute according to your means and needs.

Believe this; we are not powerless unless we believe that we are powerless. The planet is dying but we are so busy anticipating the next problem that will affect us personally, that we don't give ourselves time to calm down, see the overall picture and think logically. We are stripping the earth bare of the bounty it once gave so easily because there are too many people.

Be aware that we are hard-wired into this Universal Consciousness and nothing, not even a thought, goes unregistered. Everything is energy and every thought leaves its imprint. You might find that difficult to believe but study the principle of Quantum Physics; the mind's magnetic power is affecting the very thing that is being perceived. This is not fantasy. This is scientific fact.

For instance, you might have fantasies that if exposed, would embarrass or humiliate or even shame you, but you think that as long as it stays in your mind, that you experience it all in your fantasy, that you are doing no harm! However, science has proven that everything is energy, so thoughts are energy and can create powerful mind pictures. For a short time you live in and experience the emotion of those mind pictures; they are your reality. What if those private thoughts were, following the Law of Attraction, linking with other like-minded people in the world; people who might make them manifest, in the real world. But why should you worry? It's not your young daughter, not your young son being degraded, humiliated and emotionally damaged for life.

The fact is that no matter what you say or do, or how you try to distance yourself from the horrors and sadness on this planet, nothing will compensate for your waking up to your true identity; you are a co-creator of the quality of life on this planet. You came here with free-will and the power to change the life you are leading and so contribute to lifting the consciousness of humankind, out of the illusion of fear.

Shakespeare said: "All the world's a stage." If you left the world stage today, will you look back and regret your lack-lustre performance? Your time centre-stage on this earth is coming to an end. So stop complaining and do something to make it better - relax and smile! That's better!

PARASITE CALLED FEAR

If you think of Fear as a parasite that came to this planet eons ago and now sits mostly undetected, nibbling at our innards, then every time we get stressed, angry, worried, anxious or we anticipate trouble, it's feeding time folks! It's like dishing up a big beef steak to keep your Fear nourished! Fear relies on your 'out-of-control, imagination,' for it's very survival!

So the next time you get uptight – consider your ulcer!

(Also remember the first commandment: "I am the Lord thy God. Though shall have no other God before me?"

Well forget that one; Fear is what we pay most attention to and every time you repeat a superstition, you are making yourself subservient to a graven image; an inanimate object.

Fear can only thrive in the dark; it loves to be suppressed, lurking in the dark recesses of your mind. "Oh, I don't want to think about that," you say - but you do, because worrying had become a reflex, a habit. Fear makes you think (albeit it sublimely) that worrying is part of finding the solution. Trying not to think about 'It' means you are thinking about what you are trying not to think about! With that confused negative energy going out to the Universe – guess what you will be attracting? Even if 'It' never happens you will have spent so much of your precious life, living in dread of it! What a waste.

(Suppression is not the way to control fear. I was fortunate, with Silva Method training in self-mental and emotional discipline, I was able to clear mental baggage from the past and move on. See www.junekidd.com) Now, when negative thoughts invade, I am able to recognize them for what they are and simply withdraw my attention from these confidence-sucking negative feelings and focus on the better outcome I desire.

Fear cannot thrive in the Light; the light of investigation, of scrutiny, of exposure. So stop acting as a victim - investigate what it is that is sapping the joy from your life and become your own

34

master. Don't be a Job; "What I most feared has come to me…!"

Poor people have too many children because they need some to survive to look after parents in their old age. Those thoughts are dominated by fear and are quite understandable but there has to come a time when the consequences of overpopulation have to be faced.

Primitive man needed Fear to give the alert every time a sabre-toothed tiger came near the cave but when sabre-toothed tigers became thin on the ground and you were no longer paying it attention, Fear swapped its portfolio for 'the bullying boss, the mortgage repayments and health scares.'
You have to admire its flexibility!

Fear should no more define you, or dictate your attitude to life, than dandruff defines your physical type or state of health.

For circumstances that threaten to overwhelm you, take the advice of Sigmund

Freud: "Write it out of yourself". List everything and every permutation of the problem, one by one, then start reducing the list by clearing the simple ones first. You will be amazed how quickly you can isolate and concentrate on the central problem that needs a clear, uncluttered mind to solve it.

CHECK YOUR IDEA OF LOGIC

"To put anything right you have first to understand where you are going wrong."

Example: This man is working in an office as a problem solver, his desk covered with things to attend to as more and more emails demanding his attention. He's good at his job, working diligently and it seems logical to him to keep an eye open for any problem building on the horizon. Once spotted he can attend to them before they become big problems. He does this, covering every possible angle, because he has a dream, a dream of leaving work on a Friday with a clear tidy desk, all emails answered, the problems solved, and having a free, relaxing weekend ahead with nothing nagging at his peace of mind. So why doesn't he ever achieve it?

He doesn't ever achieve it because his main focus is on problem solving!   He's so fixated on problem solving; looking out for them, anticipating them, keeping on top of them as the answer to achieving his own dream - a free weekend - that he is attracting more problems to solve! That's where his main focus of attention is, not on his Friday night freedom! The Universal Mind picks up on his unwavering focus on problem solving - and assuming that's what the man wants more of, delivers it without judgment!

So get a grip and stop focusing on the thing you don't want to happen. Did you say that you don't? Are you sure? Well, let's examine the direction of your thoughts when dealing with crisis, be it trouble with the kids, lack of money, a health issue or uncertainty at work. Is this you when you are stressed?

"Wow, they're cutting back. I don't want to <u>lose this job</u>!"
"How will I cope if I <u>lose this job</u>?"

"If I <u>don't get another job</u>, how long can I manage <u>without an income</u>?"

"I mustn't <u>lose this job</u>"

"<u>I'll lose my house!</u>"

"I won't <u>lose this job</u>."

"<u>I can't afford</u> to <u>lose this job!</u>"

"I'm going to <u>fight to keep this job</u>."

"<u>I'll keep a look out for</u> another job."

You think that by facing the worst outcome (with a shot of defiant optimism) and making contingency plans, that this is <u>constructive thinking</u>. Right? Wrong, and you have also handed over your power and pride to fear.

The Law of Entrainment, The Universal Law of Attraction will be attracted to, and give your more of, whatever you are focusing on strongest, and in this case, your whole focus is on <u>losing your job</u>! The whimpering little bit about not wanting this to happen, hardly gets a look in, in the 'attention/energy' stakes and to crown it all, you think that by facing up to every possible

miserable outcome, you are being positive!
Let's have more examples:

"I don't want to miss the bus"
 Focus is on <u>missing the bus</u>.
"Oh God, please say I haven't got cancer."
Focus? <u>Got Cancer</u>
"Don't let the kids get into trouble"
Focus? <u>The kids in trouble</u>.
"I wish they liked me."
Focus? "<u>They don't like me</u>"
"I don't want to be so fat."
Focus? "<u>I'm fat, I'm fat, I'm fat!</u>"
(I write this from experience; I've been
through it all. And becoming aware of 'how'
you think, is key! Later, I will tell you how I
did it, how I took charge of my mind, my
out-of-control imagination and my life!)

I've underlined parts, so that you see where
your focus is. what you are attracting like a
magnet. The Universe doesn't care if you
are bad or sad, good or downright rotten; it
just delivers if you focus long enough and
strong enough. That's quite sad. Simply

because of your lack of awareness of how you are using 'The Law' your entire focus, visualization, imagination and emotion, was centred on <u>fear of a bad outcome, losing your job,</u> but putting a brave face on it.

From the start of the first rumour of redundancy, when you tried to find reassurance by bottling it up or sharing your fears with other worried workers, you and they were creating more things to worry about, and so your imagination, manipulated by Fear, became dominant. The more you worried, thinking that you were being realistic by preparing yourself for the worst, the stronger became Fears manipulative hold over you. Sometimes fear can make you impotent in every aspect – and it's all in the mind! (Another beef steak to the parasite fear, as it chomps at your innards!)

Your reaction was an ingrained habit. You fell back in the groove of worrying as a way of dealing with the situation. You gave hardly a thought to the damage you were inflicting on your nervous system or why your children's eyes were not shining. You fell back into the old groove, your felt powerless but the only difference between that groove and the grave is the depth!

Your emotions are a good early warning sign of things going wrong. Start paying attention to them and you will soon learn to steer your thoughts away from the negative, 'but what if,' for there is no end to 'but what if!'

Now, if by any luck you didn't lose your job, you and your family have still lived the misery of insecurity with you. True or false worries, Fear doesn't care. It got your full attention for that short time and it's been given enough power over you, to feed on for ages and there's always more on where that came from – if you allow it…

If you added up the months that must run into years that you have spent worrying over nothing, well, what a waste of your precious time on this planet. Not to mention the damage that stress had done to your arteries! When, by becoming aware, you could have been operating as Master of your fate.

And when you finally had the ' all-clear' from most of those past worries, I would bet big money that you never gave a quarter of the time or energy saying 'Thank you.'

So be aware that you are operating that magnet, minute-by-minute, because now you know how it works, there's no excuse. However, you do have free will to stay in the pit!

The real upside is that once you get used to monitoring, and when necessary, changing the direction of your thoughts, it will become second nature. That is when you start to reap the real reward; a confidence that you have never experienced a surety that by focusing, working towards and expecting the right outcome, you begin to create it.

There is however, a casualty. Fear loses its job, its grip on you and slowly, with lack of your attention, it will shrivel away like an old balloon left behind the sofa after Christmas…

THE PLASTIC NATURE OF 'REALITY'

Reality is as easy to manipulate as soft plastic. The difference is that you mould it with the power, not of the hand, but of the mind

Be kind to yourself. Fear and anger affect judgment, your concept of reality. What we believe to be true, right or wrong, is our reality and we make decisions based on what we believe and feel emotionally – so stop watching those soap-operas where people do nothing but cheat and shout and threaten each other. By living this daily brainwashing 'reality' your children might grow up thinking that aggression is the only way to succeed (and you might find yourself in the firing line!)

We need to get our foundations strong to protect our children. We are Masters who have to remember what we already know. That's why Jesus came here; to wake us up.

We need to commit to our full potential - our full wonderful potential.

As Jesus said: "Whatever I do, you can do – and more…"

Supporting this, the philosopher GOETHE wrote: "Until one is committed there is hesitancy, the chance to draw back, always ineffectiveness. Concerning all acts of initiative there is one element of truth, the ignorance of which kills countless ideas and splendid plans. The moment one commits oneself then providence takes over. All sorts of things occur to help one that would otherwise never have occurred. A whole stream of events issue from the decision, raising in one's favour all manner of unseen incidents and meetings and material assistance which no man would have dreamed could come his way.

Whatever you can do, or dream you can do, begin it!"

AS ABOVE - SO BELOW

No matter what we call it, every soul on earth stems from the one all-powerful source, we call God. Just as every atom in our physical bodies came from an exploding star, billions of years ago, so similarly, our souls emanate from one Devine all-powerful centre; the source of Love and Wisdom. Everyone stems from this 'Oneness.' But not everyone is aligned to it – yet. Quote Professor Jim Al-Khalili: "We are all made of stardust!" Isn't that just wonderful?

Love is ever expanding. You cannot say to someone; "You must only love me." That is like trying to hold on to a handful of sand. The tighter you grip the faster it slips through your fingers. Be assured that love has many faces and all of them good. Allow it to flourish in your life and your joy will know no bounds.

You will know that you are doing the right thing by the grace and ease with which your life flows! Love powers the Universe.

In His parables and conversations, Jesus referred constantly to the ability of the individual to connect to the 'God Source.' To understand that freedom and joy are not, 'out there.' (So there is little point in going on a spiritual journey) Our minds and imaginations are our tools to use and to command. Do not be afraid to take back control of your lives. It's never too late – or too soon!

That's why Jesus said:
"The Kingdom of God is within… (each one of us)
"Pray to your Father in Heaven." (go 'within' for the answer.)
"Whatever I do, you can do…." (Just plug into the universal power grid!)

The Emerald Tablet, circa **3000 BC**.
"**As** above, so below. **As** within, so without."

This Wisdom has been debated and accepted by the greatest minds from the beginning of recorded time.

The Hopi Indians prophecy says:
"We are the ones we have been waiting for." So why wait longer?

THE 'ONENESS'

Christians, Jews, Muslims; we all share the same *Old Testament*. The Jewish religion does not believe that Jesus was The Son of God. Christians do. The Muslim faith has great respect for Jesus but they call him a prophet.

Elaine Pagels, Professor of Religion at Princeton University, found one interpretation in the Aramaic language (spoken by Jesus) was that he actually said 'I am *a* son of God'. (Worth considering?)

So, whether he is The Son of God, or a Prophet or a very wise man preaching the power of love, our cultures are all respectful of 'the man' and his teachings, teachings that are as relevant today as over the last 2,000 years – and now, more urgent

If our individual religions believe that everything and everyone belongs to '**God**' then surely we are all offsprings, sons and daughters of The **Almighty.** What is there to argue about apart from title and the method of presentation? And is the *difference* worth going to war over? We have got so used on this planet to the horror of atrocities being inflicted on others in the name of a loving God that after a brief shudder, it passes from the memory. And that is the tragedy.

Also, if people leave their homeland because of conflict but continue that conflict from their new country, then they are abusing the hospitality of their hosts.

It is time that we, the ordinary, law abiding, family-minded, good-parenting, hard working, vast majority of any persuasion, who just want to live in harmony and get on with their lives and worship in their own way, speak out and make it known.

It really is D.I.Y time!

TIME TO BE YOUR OWN JUDGE

Trust your judgment but keep in mind that there is no single reality. The life you live is based on <u>your personal concept of reality</u> - and there are as many realities as there are people alive to create and interpret them. You are the lead player and the director in this, your own drama, your time on stage. So study and interpret, with great attention to detail, the role you have chosen to play for this lifetime and play it to its full potential - and have fun!

BENEFITS TAKE PRACTICE

Awareness and your emotions are a good indicator of how you are doing. Your success (and by success I mean your contentment with the quality of your life) will be powered by your joy and belief in your ability to help yourself, so always acknowledge your successes however small and however often. It keeps the delivery channel open.

Even if bad things happen, your attitude, your stronger, clearer thinking will lessen their impact on you and your family. Sit quietly, concentrate on your inner most centre and simply ask for direction and constructive help, give thanks at the same time as asking, <u>smile a smile of relief</u>, and balance for balance according to the energy you put into your expectation, the solution <u>will</u> be presented to you. Guaranteed.

It is interesting to read the tenet of the Royal Marine Commando Unit.

THE ROYAL MARINE COMMANDO UNIT

Laughter is a bandage.
Laughter halts fear.
Laughter staves off hunger.
Laughter keeps out the cold.
Laughter cools hot heads.
Laughter knows no language.
Laughter should be taken very seriously

Your mind is your weapon.
Your mind is a shield against fear.
Your mind can overcome hunger.
Your mind can eradicate pain.
FEAR IS A STATE OF MIND.

BULLYING: CHILDREN & ADULTS

It is vital for our children to be aware of this law of cause and effect, especially when it comes to bullying. If the child is afraid, then he will be concentrating on fear, of being hurt, of being humiliated, of being alone, of being defenseless, of his parents not being able to do much about it etc. The whole focus of its attention will be on victim status and so another child has been snared into the illusion - that we are in the hands of fate. And so this parasite called Fear will have another lifetime victim – unless we teach the children to refocus on the outcome they so passionately desire.

The Bible says: "Being kind to your enemies is like heaping burning coals on their heads."

I actually have two friends in high positions who used this technique; one worked in T.V. the other, in Hospital Administration.

Both worked for bulling (and often lying) bosses who had reduced other staff to tears.

The first, a man, having learned the technique from the Silva Method training program, just sat unprotesting as the usual abuse was directed at him. The difference on this occasion was that, calling on his training, he just relaxed and mentally sent back wave after wave of kind, understanding thoughts to this man as he ranted and raged. <u>This mental change, this refusal to be intimidated,</u> protected my friend emotionally from the onslaught. After a few minutes, his boss seemed baffled by the lack of response and gradually his words dried up – and he then turned and walked out of the office! Everyone there, who had witnessed his previous outrageous attacks, expressed sheer amazement! He had never just given up before. From then on, there was no more bullying! But the key was, my friend's change of attitude.

My other friend, a woman I shall call 'D', who successfully ran a hospital department for a number of years, suddenly found every decision she made challenged and ridiculed by a new female colleague.

The unfounded criticism became a daily occurrence until 'D', reduced to tears, was considering handing in her notice. Things then came to a head and a meeting was arranged; the woman, 'D' and 'D's' immediate boss. The other woman came into the meeting, 'on the attack' and didn't stop – but during the non-stop onslaught, something strange happened - 'D' suddenly found that she didn't care! The words no longer upset her, she felt no need to defend herself and began to physically relax! Meeting over, 'D' stood up and said to her boss, "She has been telling lies for the last half an hour. It's up to you if you want to do something about it."

As it happened, the woman decided to leave almost immediately! However, as I pointed out to 'D' – the big change came when you changed your attitude to this woman. Your decision gave you a protective barrier; one that the woman would have sensed, one that immediately neutralised her power.

(Teasing or winding someone up and saying it is all 'part of the game' and that there is 'no harm in it' is another form of bullying. It is at the very least, unkind, and can end in some tragic cases with children killing themselves. No harm in it?)

HELPING HAND

Some people can't be helped to move on with their lives because they are not yet ready; they need to ferment for a little longer; stew in their own juice... Playing victim is their security, the security of their insecurity, something they can rely on because they are convinced that sometime, someone or something will let them down. They call it being realistic. They expect it, look out for it, focus on it, interpret almost everything into that possible outcome - and that's what they get to keep! Frustratingly, for anyone trying to help, (because they rarely tell you to actually go away) that's their choice, their free will and they have every right to keep it - but not the right to expect you to be available everytime they want a pick-up or someone to moan at.

In the extreme, even if they choose to put their power into the hands of someone who humiliates them, they will hang onto that thread like a security blanket; that dreadful relationship, that miserable job, those unkind friends, and they will argue with a victims resigned sigh that they have 'tried to move on but can't do it - by themselves.' (But keep on trying because I like the attention!) These people need help; they say they want help – as long as they don't actually have to do anything to make the change. They don't mind <u>you</u> exhausting yourself trying to dishing up 'happy days,' but don't expect any in return.

"You can't be happy <u>all</u> of the time." That's the usual response (rather like very fat people say "I wouldn't want to be thin.") They will argue with you all day, to defend their limited expectations and you will annoy them if your argument starts to threaten their tight grip on a miserable security. "It's alright for you, you live your life 'up-there' but I'm staying down here. It's not so far to fall!"

Sometimes it demands just too much of your energy to be worth carrying on. They need to stay down there until it gets so boring (they have been boring others for years) or so awful that even they can't stand the pits any longer; usually when they realize that they've exhausted everyone's sympathy and that no one is paying them attention anymore. Then, with free will, they might decide to get out and up and join you in what is obviously an easier life. So enjoy being who you are and show how your attitude is enriching your life. That's the best and only true way to convert.

Jesus summed it up by saying:
"Don't cast your pearls before swine," After performing a miracle to help someone he said: **"Tell no man of this."**
Why? What does it mean?
Well, think how powerful and elevated you feel when you have a grand idea, or have met someone who you believe will help lift you out of your present difficulties. But

sometimes, their reaction is based on envy of your possible success.

"Have you seen the opposition? – It's been tried before – I think it's rubbish." Or in the case of a miracle: "You must have imagined it – it's just coincidence – it would have happened anyhow.

'Your confidence, that elation, the powerful energy you felt, can be drained by their negativity. That is what Jesus meant when he said: "Don't tell anyone of this. Don't lay your pearls (your joy or aspirations?) before uncaring and sometimes jealous people for rather like the 'swine' they will not value them, dismiss your hopes and undermine your confidence. Keep them close where they can flourish until they are strong enough to face opposition. You wouldn't sew delicate seeds where the fine new shoots could be trampled over.

J.K. Rowling, in her delightful book, The Tales of Beedle the Bard, wrote *"Nothing is a surer sign of weak magic than a weakness for none magical company."* Don't dismiss these wise words for if you seek the company of people who lack enthusiasm for life, it is the same as settling for 'non-magical' company. You are worth more than that!

YOUR TIME - CENTRE STAGE

William Shakespeare said: "All the world is a stage and all the men and women merely players"

Life is like choosing to see a film. <u>You</u> decide if you want to watch/live the horror movie or the comedy, or a safe (from emotion) documentary. You pay money and in doing that (by your free will) you accept that what you see on the screen will engage your emotions and become reality for you – until the lights come on.

It's rather like life on this planet. You've chosen this lifetime to learn, to get stronger and to get wiser.

Every problem comes with its own solution; sometimes not at all agreeable. but still the right thing to do.

No experience is ever wasted; you do well to remember those experiences!

But now it is time to turn the lights on, time to wake up and find out if your judgment has been sound. Do this before you depart this 'mortal coil,' and still have time to ask yourself (in the slightly misquoted words of Oliver Cromwell - "In the name of Christ, might *I* not be wrong?")

With hindsight, you might have a chance to put things right, avoiding karma and landing back here, without your previous school report! (Could do better?)

This planet is governed by illusion and Fear, and you <u>accepting</u> Fear with a sigh, as a daily fact of life, will not weaken it, or make you, stronger. At the very best, it can leave you numb to the cries of the children…

Tick tock, tick tock… Your time for leaving the stage is getting closer…

MASTER OF YOUR DESTINY

Quote: Confucius "Some people say they can do it, some people say they can't do it. They are both right because they will get what they ask for." (The Law of Attraction)

To concentrate on one objective, you have to have stillness in your life. It's no use throwing your hands up and saying you haven't got time to breath, let alone a time to do nothing - that's your old way of thinking, refusing to go forward and arguing to justify and keep its limitations and its hold on you. Now, I'm not asking you to sit cross-legged in a darkened room, trying to think of nothing for hours on end. I'm saying that two or three times a day you could get into the habit of relaxing your body from head to toe and using that peaceful time to focus on and protect your aims.

When you are relaxed and your mind is still then focus on what you want to happen and start to live the experience as though it had actually happened, as though it is your current reality. If it's a new place to live then visualize it and furnish it and see the colours you want to use. Sit in the chairs and feel what it's like to have achieved your ambition.

Don't get hung up about 'being selfish' for wanting things for yourself. Once you are in the manifesting zone, you can bring things into your life that will benefit others too. Just do the work first. Believe you can do it and you can do it. Jesus said so! Oh, and say thank you, as soon as you have sent your project thoughts out into the ether.

To manifest, you need to develop powerful mental focus and the most efficient time to do this is when you have silence within and preferably without. You could start practicing right now and also make it a ritual at bedtime, when you wake in the morning or in the middle of the night. Just two or three minutes, practiced regularly, is a good start.

I used to have what I called a butterfly mind, darting from one subject to another and wearing myself out. Fortunately, I graduated in The Silva Method in 1986, and I can now go into a 30 second fully-aware, deep mental and physical relaxation (and stay upright) while looking at the tinned tomatoes in the supermarket! Rapid, deep relaxation is so therapeutic! To be master of your destiny you have first to develop a strong mind, one that will stay focused, and think clearly, particularly in an emergency. Developing a strong mind is central to Silva Method training and the key to its success for more than fifty years. Using the Silva Method, I, a dyslexic writer, also learned to spell virtually overnight at the age of 40. You will find details in the last part of my book, *Unshriven,* and in this book, headed; 'A Life Enriched by Silva'.

MANIFESTING

To gain confidence in your ability to manifest an outcome, start the process in a simple fun way at first, with little things; catching the train, getting that bargain, activating green lights all the way, getting that parking space, that contact calling you.

Concentrate, concentrate, focus, visualize, live the moment, feel your smile when you see the lights change to green, time and again. Don't harbour any doubt and every time you get a good result, take a moment to say a powerful, 'thank you.' This two-way acknowledgement is extremely powerful and acknowledges your part in the success and belief that 'it' will be delivered. Remember to say 'thank you' as soon as you have made the request and assume that you have it. I find that when my diary is too full or when I have conflicting appointments that I can't sort out, I just look up, close my eyes for a moment and say "Over to you", followed by "Thank you." I assure you that 100% of the time, people call to cancel or move times and everything works out right. This is because I know it will; no doubt whatsoever and that is the key. Having no doubt!

HEALTH

Stress is a killer. Not the kind of stress that
flits in and out of our daily life - we are
designed to cope with that - but <u>unremitting</u>
stress, the kind you can't see a way out of.
The kind that sucks you dry mentally,
emotionally and physically, dominating your
every waking moment. Fearful worrying
thoughts of problems without an apparent
solution are sending weakening messages to
your body, to your cells, to your immune
system.

Cancer is a word, not a life sentence.

Sayings like "It's worrying me to death, I
can't get it out of my mind, I can't think
straight, it's beaten me," will only serve to
make you feel even more powerless.

If (for instance), your <u>unremitting</u> stress is
the result of someone else's problems, be
kind to yourself and know when it is time to

let go. The fact is that you cannot live another person's life for them. You don't have the ability or the right. Stop the Gulliver complex of putting the hooks of other people's expectations into your emotional body. Instead, start to visualize what changes you desire. Re-examine your way of life. How can it be altered? There is always an alternative.

If you have tried unsuccessfully all the obvious avenues for help, then my tried and tested advice is to 'hand it over!' Just close your eyes, state the problem, *once only*, then with complete confidence, knowing that the Universal Mind is always open for new orders, hand it over. Say. 'Thank you,' when you make the request, assume it's fixed and leave it to the powers that be.

(If you are already saying 'That won't work' then it won't!)

Einstein: Unless at first an idea seems absurd – then there is no hope for it.

DEVELOPING A STRONG MIND

"Nothing in the world can take the place of
persistence.
Talent by itself will not; nothing is more
common than the unsuccessful man with
talent. Genius will not; unrewarded genius is
almost a proverb. Education will not; the
world is full of educated derelicts.
*Persistence and determination together are
omnipotent?*

Anon

THROUGH THE EYES OF A CHILD

For those of you who see evil in the word magic and in stories of Father Christmas or Harry Potter by J.K. Rowling, I suggest you ponder the words of a young boy, speaking on T.V. Rescued, after being held hostage by fundamentalists in his school room in Beslam, he and his class mates were threatened with death by shooting if they dared to move:

"I kept still very still and thought of Harry Potter and his invisible cloak. I just kept thinking of him and of keeping still and I knew he would come and rescue me."

And as is stated in the Bible (and from very many other learned sources) "Whatsoever you ask for in prayer, BELIEVE you have it and you have it."

(It is not necessary to place your hands closed or open to pray, it just has to be sincere thought. This child was praying for someone he knew was on the side of Good.) His unwavering belief that Good could overcome evil, that he believed he would be saved because Harry Potter was working for Good - was beyond simple faith. So ask yourself, would a loving God condemn the act of saving a child, just because it came from an unconventional source?

Surely the source of all Goodness is Divine. It does and should filter through us all for manifestation in daily life. Why do we keep expecting God to do it all for us? Look for the good in humankind and you will find the good.

"And what if," you cynics may say, "he had got shot?" Well, better to live in hope than die in despair. Even if he had been murdered, the child would have been saved many hours of sheer terror and that's got to be worth a lot.

So, however it was done, however it came

about, that child was delivered to safety when others were shot. That boy's single-minded focus not only kept him alive but shielded him from a lifetime of emotional damage, as other children were traumatized and murdered in front of him. You see, no one had undermined his belief in the magic of possibilities; no one had told him otherwise. (The miracles of Jesus must have seemed like the magic of a magician to most who witnessed them). No one had told the boy that it was nonsense to believe in things you couldn't see or touch, or that magic just didn't exist - so his <u>unwavering focus was on rescue</u>. He truly believed, as you believe, so it is for you!

If J.K. Rowling does nothing else wonderful in her life, she did her full quota by keeping this little boy's attention away from terror and switching it on to hope; an attitude of mind that will help him throughout life. A child's unwavering belief in goodness is powerful indeed!

WHAT IS KARMA?

So what is Karma? Karma, to use the vernacular, is getting back what you put in, reaping what you sow, what goes round comes round, not only getting your comeuppance but also the just reward and benefits for the good you have done. It's like money saved in the bank – or like an overdraft!

Karma is your destiny determined by your actions, and can be carried through from lifetime to lifetime until resolved. If, for instance, you have relationships that turn out badly every single time, where do you think the 'always turns out the same' is coming from? Give a thought that it is probably coming from you. It is some unresolved problem that your spirit soul will not let you by-pass until it is resolved. You are attracting this totally unsuitable person or situation and you will continue to do this until the problem is faced and resolved. If you don't do it in this lifetime, you will face it in the next.

This is the craziness with the system of life and rebirth and Karma. We come back into this world with no memory of past lives, hopefully with an instinct for better judgement, but faced with having to learn right from wrong, all over again! By the time we've got the hang of 'what goes round comes round,' and have cleared up the debts from a past life, we've probably clocked up a whole load more Karma, which means we have to come back again - and so it goes on because we are not aware that we are creating our destiny as we go!

Most references to the working of Karma were removed from the Holy Bible on a direct order from the Emperor Justinian at Constantinople in the year 553 AD. He and his wife Theodora ran a self indulgent and tyrannical regime and didn't like the idea of paying for it in future lifetimes.

But, not believing the truth doesn't make the truth untrue.

KARMA, THE THEOSOPHICAL SOCIETY & SCIENCE OF MIND

Various philosophical organisations have developed and rationalised the idea of karma, these include:

Madam Helena Blavatsky, in 1875, was one of three founder members of the society, who strove to form a nucleus of the universal brotherhood of humanity, without distinction of face, creed, sex, cast or colour.

The Theosophical Society includes the study of Art, Religion, Science and Philosophy. Most members believe that Humanity evolves through a series of stages, visualized by a series of concentric circles, the centre being the most enlightened and Karma-free.

No member has any authority to impose their views on any other member and so all are able to explore possibilities presented by other enquiring minds.

Central to this philosophy is the belief that thoughts and subsequent actions affect future development on the path to freedom. Like attracts Like. Karma!

SCIENCE OF MIND

The founder of the Science of Mind, **Dr. Eearnest Holmes**, is recognised today as one of the leading viewpoints in modern metaphysics and new thought. He once said:

> "We look forward to the day when science and religion shall walk hand in hand through the visible and the invisible."

To suppose that the Creative Intelligence of the universe would create man in bondage and leave him bound, would be to dishonour the Creative Power we call God. The Highest God and the Innermost God is one God. We have self-will and self-determination. This grants us the power and with it the responsibility to make or break our world through the workings of our minds.

BUDDHISM

Buddhism also uses the mental pattern of concentric circles as the symbolic path to Enlightenment. Reaching the inner point, one is considered Karma free and able to escape further lifetimes on earth.

The 4th Dalai Lama once said: "Each individual is master of his or her destiny: it is up to each person to create the cause of happiness."

MY LIFE ENRICHED BY SILVA

'Life is strange! We seem to go along the same track with no real thought of dramatic change and then one action, one decision, the meeting with one person that seems like sheer coincidence can change our lives like the turn of a coin – but as Jose Silva often said:

"Call them coincidences and you will be amazed how many coincidences there are."

Living in Saudi Arabia, 6,000 miles away from my home in England, this is the story of my 'turning point' and a most remarkable chain of 'coincidences,' that introduced me to The Silva Method and eventually, to my writing this book.

PERFECT TIME – PERFECT PLACE

I had left the pace and excitement of working in and around New York City to be married in New Orleans. Then with my husband (a physician working in Saudi Arabia) we flew from the Deep South, caught a flight to London, said hello and goodbye to friends and family, collected my entry visa then raced to Heathrow to board a flight to the Middle East! Once aboard we relaxed, cosseted in large comfortable seats, soft Arabic music, fat dates and sweet mint tea served from tiny cups. Sit back, enjoy, the pressure is over.

We arrived some six hours later to the call for evening prayer echoing from minaret to minaret, a backdrop of purple pink sky and a sun sinking rapidly into an indigo sea, spilling its gold across the horizon like the pricked yolk of a magnificent egg. This was the view from a picture window of my new home. There was no evening time, no gentle fading of the light. The day just collapsed into night - an Arabian night and, silhouetted in the last of the stretching rays, a man riding a camel out into the silence of the desert. It was a scene that was to become so familiar but one that never lost its magic.

Stepping out of the plane the humidity of the city engulfed me like a soft mist - and I loved it! Time had come to a halt. Time had gone backwards. Here they used the Hijra calendar. The year was 1403.

Welcome to Jeddah. Welcome to the Kingdom of Saudi Arabia.

WHEN THE STUDENT IS READY
THE TEACHER APPEARS

I had established a routine, programming myself to wake in the early hours of the morning, (every morning!) to direct healing energies and prayers to a dear friend living in England. She had been ill for a long time, the prognosis was not good, and my prayers were as much about keeping her comfortable and calm, as for a miraculous healing.

From past experiences I was utterly convinced of the power of mental telepathy. I had been told by my friend and yoga teacher that 2 a.m. was a good time to communicate (that part of sleep when a person is most relaxed) but as the Middle East was two hours ahead, I would set my alarm clock to go off just before 4 a.m. Struggling to surface and then dragging myself out of bed, I would have to spend the next ten minutes or so pacing round and round the sitting room, making myself wake up so that I could concentrate on my friend's needs without yawning or wanting to lie down again. The difficulty was that once the mental work was done, I couldn't get back to sleep. One morning as dawn broke, reaching the point of mental and physical exhaustion, I looked Heavenwards and said, "I really cannot do this any longer. I need some help!"

I spoke these words with the <u>utter conviction</u> that I was <u>entitled</u> to help and that I could expect delivery. It was in a good and just cause and I had done all that I could do, unaided, believing as I did that 'God helps those who help themselves'. Please do notice the emphasis: I <u>expected</u> to receive help. I did not hold <u>any</u> thought of doubt or refusal. I gave no energy to fear and I wasn't suppressing anxiety for I had none. Even so, I could not have anticipated the speed of delivery!

By a strange coincidence(?) an English woman, Jennifer E., who had married an Egyptian doctor and emigrated from England to Australia, had arrived in Saudi Arabia with her husband who was to work at our hospital. Three days after she entered the Kingdom and just hours after I had asked for help Jennifer knocked on my door. I can't remember or even now imagine why Jennifer came to see me, but I found myself explaining to this complete stranger why I was in such a weary state and not very good company.

Jennifer, a really bright, bubbly person, always smiling (she never changed in all the time I knew her) said without hesitation, "You should take the 'Silva Mind Control' training course." (The name was later changed as it could have been misinterpreted.) "Self control over your sleeping pattern is just one of the many techniques you will be taught," she continued as I made coffee. "How to put yourself to sleep, how to wake up on time without a clock and, very importantly for you, through developing your creative visualisation you will also be taught how to use your mental energy to direct healing energies to anyone, anywhere in the world. It's only what you are doing now," she laughed, reading the doubt on my face, "But you can do it without exhausting yourself. Jose Silva, says: "You should do as your doctor instructs but help him and help your body to heal by using the power of your mind."

It was only on reflection that I realised that the timing of Jennifer's visit was the <u>first</u>, the start of a chain of the most unbelievable 'coincidences,' that were to change the direction of my life and unlock aptitudes I would never have credited myself with. Now, amazingly, this chain of 'coincidences' began to fall into place, one after the other like a line of dominos. The <u>second</u> 'coincidence' was that the name 'SILVA,' rang a bell. I seemed to recall a friend in England saying that she had taken 'Silva' training and had spoken highly of it. <u>Third</u>, as luck (?) would have it, I was already booked to fly home that week! (It was as though Universal Intelligence was one step ahead of me, knowing what I needed, organising the moves and providing the back up!)

<u>Fourth</u>: The day I arrived back in England I telephoned my friend. "Yes, I have done the Silva training and I can't recommend it highly enough. It changed my life. <u>It just so happens</u> that there is a seminar in London this next weekend with an introductory meeting on Friday evening. I'm free. Would you like to go?" (Would I like to go? You wanna play me at dominos?)

MY INTRODUCTION TO THE
SILVA METHOD

That Friday evening two friends and I sat in the conference room of a smart London hotel, every seat taken (most surprisingly) by almost equal numbers of men and women listening intently to the introductory talk given by Paul Fransella. Paul, medium height, late middle aged, dark hair, passionate about his subject, animated as he talked, eyes so intense that they held your full attention as he explained the totally logical thinking behind the method. "The training will teach you how to direct the power of your own imagination, visualising only the outcome you desire, giving no attention to fearful thinking and lack of success. The power of your mind is enormous. I am here to teach you how to harness and direct that power. You will learn how to unlock the power of creative visualisation, and how to use your mind in a 'special way,' a way that can <u>direct</u> and

<u>receive</u> information. You have the innate ability to direct and improve our lives by simply taking charge of our way of thinking." (Silva Method handbook, "Tapping the secrets of Your Mind for Total Self Mastery")

What Paul was saying was to most of us revolutionary and very exciting. We all wanted to know more and at the end of the talk I joined the queue and signed up without any hesitation. What I had heard made total and logical sense. Everything begins with a thought, so my being able to control the direction of my thinking must be beneficial. (No more lying in bed telling myself I couldn't get back to sleep.) Three points had convinced me that this was an honourable organization, with integrity, its maxim.

1) I was to be taught how to work for MY self-empowerment and for the <u>'Betterment of Mankind'</u> (and not for some brain washing 'ology', demanding my

94

unquestioning subservience with the ultimate aim of extracting a regular (and unearned) income from my bank balance.)

2) We were reminded, 'You can reject anything we say, at any level of the mind,' so no one was going to try and manipulate my subconscious mind.

3) Surprisingly in a money orientated world we were told: 'Once you have graduated, you can take the course again, free of charge, anywhere in the world, for the rest of you life.' Even now we pay only a minimal fee to cover overheads.

I had signed up and paid for training that was to benefit every aspect of my life - but if I had thought that I was to sit back, listen to the instruction and get a quick fix-it-all, I was in for a sharp awakening.

DAY ONE INTRODUCTION

Jose Silva spent 22 years developing techniques that would allow us to use the power of imagination and mind and access unused parts of the brain, and in developing this programme, and we were in good company.

<u>Einstein</u>: "Knowledge is wonderful but imagination is everything."

<u>Richard Bach</u>, author of Jonathan Livingstone Seagull, and Illusions, the adventures of a reluctant Messiah, wrote: <u>"Whatever you can visualise, you can actualise."</u>

On that first day we were reassured by the science, philosophy, (with your new powers will come a responsibility to use them "for the betterment of mankind.") and practical application of the programme, and by the end of that first morning we were confidently beginning to direct the focus of attention by using deeper levels of our minds.

This was a to be a learned discipline that would to enable us to take control of things such as: unwanted habits, pain control and the quickening of healing, and stimulate intuition (amazing!) so that our 6th sense would become a creative and problem solving part of daily life. With all this, we were assured, we would achieve a cheerful inner peace, a quiet optimism, confident that we are more in control of our lives than we ever imagined. (This would prove to be absolutely true!)

Then we were instructed in a number of exercises but repeatedly told: "You are in control of your own mind and imagination. They are your powerful mental tools. You can disregard anything we say at any level of the mind. You are always in control."
And of course, we were; that was the whole point; we had to do the work for ourselves.

(It is a fact that anyone or any organization that wants to take control of your sovereignty; take away your free will to decide, is not working for your benefit. It usually comes down to either an obsessive desire to control another – or more and regular cash deposits in their bank! As you will see, this is not the way that the Silva organization works.)

The training continued: Now, visualize improved health, your key to success, fulfillment, your personal development. Relax deeper, take charge of your thinking. Relax, go deeper, concentrate, meditate, visualize, focus your mind.

It didn't stop! But by the end of that first day I was really getting the hang of it. No daydreaming in these classes, they were too exciting. I went to bed that night quite worn out - and I was awake again at the usual time, just as I had been in Saudi! The difference now was in my attitude. I was motivated to succeed. I felt that I was in charge and I absolutely **expected** to stop this cycle of sleep deprivation.

Sitting up I said to myself, 'I totally believe in the power of my mind and of this training. It's got to work because it's so logical. I've travelled thousands of miles to get here and I've paid for this instruction. It's got to work! Payment is always a motivating factor. People do not value what comes free! Concentrating on my Sleep Control lesson I must have been asleep in seconds! I woke the next morning at 7.30 on the dot as I had told myself to do (another lesson well learned) feeling totally refreshed, invigorated, energized, and confident in my ability to embrace all that this method had to offer. I was delighted with my early accomplishment, the potential seemed unlimited and this was only after the first day of the Basic Course! Here I was, taking control of my mind and my body, already expecting and getting results - and all that was required was my attention!

DAY TWO

We started the day without preamble and, after a brief recap, began to build on yesterday's sound structure, filling the morning with headache, weight and smoking control. Then came mental house cleaning, becoming aware of and freeing our mind from old inhibiting blockages. Interspersed with meditation, visualization and strengthening focus of the mind, this was proving to be another amazing day. Rapid relaxation followed, a strong mental tool in an emergency or any stressful situation. After lunch came rapid learning, sharper memory, happier relationships, the attaining of new goals then meditation and an amazing session on dream control and how to remember and record them.

That demanding day ended with a lesson on how to prepare for, and take exams, how to sharpen the memory (going back in time and recall exact details from books), remember lists of things up to 100, and so very much more. We were discovering just some of the many mental powers that are ours by birthright such as our ability to send and receive information, and receive help and guidance on any subject. Call it Divine Intelligence, or the Universal Mind, or whatever you are comfortable with but direct your attention to the highest and purest possible source.

And so another wonderful, satisfying, exhausting day came to an end but our most amazing achievement was yet to come…

THE LAST EXERCISE OF THE FINAL COURSE

On this last day the air buzzed with excitement and confidence was high. The work we had done on self-improvement was already showing results. We all had experiences to relate, and the energy in that room was palpable. We were elated and totally convinced that the programme was working. Using the techniques we had practiced and were by now very easy, we put ourselves rapidly into a depth of relaxation, to a point where the individual can overcome pain in things like dentistry. For me, the energy of intense concentration manifested itself in the form of increasing pressure, like the push of a thumb in the middle of my eyebrows, the feeling becoming stronger the deeper my relaxation. There was no point in pretending or making things up. If we didn't give it our attention we would only be depriving ourselves of our every expanding potential.

By this time we were coming to the end of the day and I found myself working on two levels, my mind sharp and focused but my body relaxed to a point where, as long as I didn't move, I felt detached from it. I wasn't aware of my hands or feet and had no idea in what position I had left them. (Some people have perfected this technique to a point when they can undergo dental surgery without anesthetic.) But, should any emergency present, we had been taught to be wide-awake and ready to act in an instant. Even at this level, we were in charge at all times for while the mind and body were occupied, the subconscious mind, like a protective overseer, was always alert. It is a truly wonderful experience to be so deeply relaxed.

On to the last exercise on the last day, a culmination of all the work we had done. It was designed to strengthen our belief and faith in our ability to use the power of the mind to diagnose physical problems and then to mentally project healing. This was close to my heart as 'absent healing,' had brought Jennifer and the Silva Method, into my life. All that we, a room full of eager students, were told was the age, the sex, and the location of the person that our instructor Paul, had in mind, a 12 year old boy, living in California.

We were then told to take ourselves down to the inner conscious level, concentrate on the given facts and wait. Almost instantly a mental picture began to emerge, fuzzy at first but gradually clearing and then I saw him, a boy, dark curly hair, walking towards me on a beach. The only puzzling thing was that his right leg was shimmering from the hip line, to the ground. That was all.

After a few minutes we ended our meditations and were asked what we had visualised. It was quite startling when other people in that room began to repeat my exact experiences. Others had slight variations on the same picture.

Then Paul told us that the boy in question had had a high hip leg amputation when he was only two years old! I looked around the room at the expressions of amazement and incredulity. How mind-blowing was that! This was the power of the 'directed' mind. It surely knows no man-made boundaries. I said goodbye to my friends and left London, giving silent thanks to this man, Jose Silva, and his training programmer that had put me in charge of my butterfly mind and free-wheeling imagination, expanding my horizons to a point of liberating excitement! With a lot of theory and some actual experience under my belt I felt confident but little did I know that my confidence and new found beliefs would be challenged that very night!

****

Just before I got off the train, out of the blue, I felt that I had been hit in the eye with a ball – a very hard ball! The pressure and pain were frightening. It was late on Sunday night, I was alone, not registered with a doctor in UK. In desperation, as soon as I got indoors, I telephoned one of the friends with who I had taken the Silva course. She had left London at the same time and would, I hoped, be home by now. She had had experience of using the healing techniques and I knew she would help me. (Absent healing!)

'And I'm frightened,' I said, after I had explained my problem. "I can hear that." Her voice was calm. "Now I want you to put down the telephone and go into rapid deep relaxation. You know the method for healing. I will meet you at a meditative level and work with you. With two of us sending the right mental pictures and combining energies, it will be very powerful." Putting the telephone down I went to work, putting into practice all that I had learned, following the procedure stage by stage and finally visualising healing. I finished by placing a hand over my eye, concentrating on that healing and visualising the outcome I so desired. My concentration was total, motivated by the very human instinct of self-preservation. I don't know how long I sat there, five minutes, fifteen? Then a strange sensation like a rapid unrelenting tapping came over the whole eye area – and when it stopped, my eye was healed! The pain had completely gone and I was breathless with relief! I had no explanation for the sensation, no one had mentioned it, so I had to accept it as 'one of those things,' and I had no reason to think of it again for many years…

SEVERAL YEARS LATER

A great air of excitement. Jose Silva was in London personally conducting the Advanced Course of the method. I was intrigued to hear him declare, "I have made a sound, electronically, that works to stimulate the body's natural immune system."

Then, placing a tape in the recording machine on the table for us all to see, he went on to tell us of the successes he had had by using it dedicatedly on very difficult health cases. "If you have a health problem you should always do as your doctor advises but you can greatly help the body to heal itself by relaxing and meditating, focusing on the outcome you desire, as you have been taught. This Silva Sound will greatly assist you. For a serious illness you should use this for fifteen minutes, three times a day and, where possible, play this sound close to the body."

He then pressed the start key – and I nearly fell off my chair!

The sound I was hearing, the Silva Sound, was the audio version of the tapping sensation that I had experienced when meditating on the healing of my eye all those years ago! I knew this sound and I knew it worked! The threat to my eyesight had been a motivating factor that had sent me into a really deep and instant meditation. I had concentrated on healing then, with total belief in my ability to instruct my body to heal itself. In those few silent minutes I had worked in another powerful dimension of awareness. By believing in my ability and right to access and receive help, I had received the benefits. My respect and admiration for Jose Silva, already high now went up to the rafters of the sky as he went on to talk of the power of the mind.

Our minds! And all that it required was our attention!

However, at the time of my first experience of self-healing, my meeting with Jose and this most remarkable repeating of the healing Silva-Sound lay several years in the future.

GHOST WRITER: "UNSHRIVEN"

The Silva Course was over and my time in England was at an end but heading back to the Middle East, the teachings of the method occupied my thoughts for most of the six-hour flight. I was filled with an inner excitement that was hard to contain. Mental barriers had become opportunities and the possibilities were breathtaking. I was surging with energy from this most extraordinary teaching, keen to make my new techniques part of my daily life. What fun! How far could the boundaries be pushed? What was I, and what was mankind in general, capable of? It was as though someone was telling me to

"Get on with it. Move forward!"

I didn't go out to work and so with the luxury of time on my hands, I had the urge to write again. I had published before but always articles or short stories for magazines, newspapers or the B.B.C. This was different however. I was developing the outline of an intriguing plot that was, I assumed, pure fiction: Set in deep countryside, a small terrace of old cottage close to Stratford-upon-Avon. The date was August 1963, and it was to be a tale of interweaving relationships and historical village detection.

Every morning as my husband drove to the hospital, I would put my 'office' out on the patio but before reading yesterday's work or touching the keys, I would do my first directed meditation of the day: deep relaxation (It is a wonderful experience to be so deeply relaxed) then distant healing, and guidance, and protection for family and friends. Once this was completed and in a light trance, I would turn my attention to 1963 and my developing novel.

Then one day, almost imperceptibly, the date began to change. Still August, still the location and cottages - but the year was now

<u>1663 and I was following the lives of two sisters!</u>

The story presenting itself from that period was fascinating and would not be dismissed and I finally decided to weave it into my 1963 version, as a 'past life,' recalled by one of my modern characters, a clairvoyant. Once I had made the decision, the two dates seemed to parallel each other; developing and interacting with ease. Writing was a joy and there were no distractions. Shaded by bougainvillea and oleander trees with a cooling breeze from the ocean, I typed as though in a light trance, my fingers on the keys, interpreting the scenes that came clearly to my mind's eye. (I had no idea at that time that this was the start of my channeling previously uncollated historic factual information from the 17th century and that once I had all of the facts, I would be calling on the services of an ordained minister of the church, to 'right the wrong.')

Gradually a pattern began to present itself, helping me decide on the day's work and as long as I stayed in this light trance with no distractions, the typed words just poured out across the pages. No writer's block for me. I sometimes had difficulty keeping up with the speed of changing situations.

Hour after hour I sat at my desk, the scenes sharp in my mind's eye, words the characters spoke, silent but clear within my thinking as my fingers raced across the keyboard. It was as though my head and my hands on the keyboard were working together and I had no awareness of my physical body. So completely immersed in the drama, (sounds, smells, sights, conversations) so driven was I, that I didn't notice the backache or tired eyes. I was on a mission. It had become personal. I was taking sides and felt the need to expose the facts about this historic and outrageous miscarriage of justice that had blighted the life of the survivors. It was really demanding work, physically, mentally and emotionally but it was exciting and I thrived on it. To work this way was my decision. When a subject or topic for that day was finished and had run its course, the thoughts, the permutations just stopped abruptly, like turning off the electricity. It happened in exactly the same way when the story finally ended, abruptly, like an empty vessel, there was nothing left. It was the end.

Had I not persevered, had I not developed daily the mental and emotional disciplines and the techniques taught by The Silva Method, "Unshriven" could never have been written. But "Unshriven" was written and published as it was meant to be!

My Silva training has enabled me to use the power of my mind to develop my five senses – and my sixth! I have had some amazing experiences and I promise you that there follows a true account of just a few:

MIND OVER MATTER

Busy all day preparing to sail our boat over to France, that night, helping keep watch I hardly closed my eyes. Into Le Havre next morning and with so much to do there was no time to sleep; checking in with the authorities, getting the boat ready for several months of idly cruising rivers and waterways leading ultimately to the Seine and Paris and the added pressure of my immediate return to England on the next ferry to return a hired sea going life raft. A 48 hour turn around and I would be back in France to start yet another adventure.

The return was long and tiring and tedious but docking in Portsmouth at midnight, I still had to get the life raft into the office for transport the next morning and then face a three-hour drive home!

It was after one in the morning when I finally cleared customs and headed for the car park. The place was deserted but I stayed on alert, striding confidently, head erect, showing no sign of my utter weariness (It's mostly vulnerable people get attacked.) but sitting in my car, relaxed at last, my shoulders sagged and I could have slept the night away. Unfortunately I didn't have a choice, as I had to get home that night, but then as luck would have it, a kindly passing taxi driver showed me the way out of Portsmouth and onto the road I needed. Waving goodbye I headed into the darkness of the countryside and the start of a drive that demanded total concentration – and then it hit me; unsteady vision and a body that demanded I rest. But I couldn't rest, not here, not in this narrow dark country lane and it was then that I called on my Silva training. Three fingers together I went 'down to level' in five seconds. (Five to one method) At that level I told myself: "When I open my eyes I will be wide awake, feeling the way I feel when I wake from a deep, restful, refreshing sleep. I will drive home with total concentration and I will not feel tired until I put the key in my front door." I visualized the process as I made the plan, actually living it, feeling my focus of attention on a drive that would be pleasant and easy. Then I counted myself out of level, snapped my fingers and felt – on top form! I did that three hour drive without any sign of stress, parked the car in my drive as I had visualized and as I turned the key in the front door – my legs almost gave way under me and I staggered to the bed and passed out, still in my clothes.

The key to my accomplishment was motivation, absolute focus and my total belief that, with my training, I had the power to meet this challenge. I was using the Law of Attraction and that is what Silva is based on and this is what Jesus taught; that the power is within us all, and we will be empowered by our successes, that we are more than we think we are and capable of more than we ever imagined.

If I had had any doubt, it would have sapped my confidence, I couldn't have driven home that night and asleep behind the wheel in a narrow lane in pitch-black darkness... who knows...

RAPID ASSESMENT

We had been on the boat in France for several months just touring the canals and rivers. During that utterly peaceful time, I did a lot of writing and one morning, deep in my work, my husband called to say we were coming into a marina and would I take the ropes and tie the boat up.

It was raining very slightly but preoccupied, I didn't thinking to change my slippery shoes. On deck I took the rope, jumped over as I always did - and my feet skidded from beneath me! Bang, I went down on to the base of my spine, my legs straddling both sides of the narrow wooden pontoon. It was a terrific shock and I felt my body react; shock waves going through me like huge waves – but literally within seconds, I went into 'Silva Mode.'

Mentally I did a rapid check of my body to see that nothing was broken. Having established that, I took charge of my thinking: O.K, no real damage so there is no need for you (my body) to send pain. Calm down.

By this time my husband was pulling me to my feet and into the boat where I lay down on the cockpit seat, still in Silva mode. Looking at his worried face I said, "Feel my pulse." It was absolutely normal! Then I noticed that both of my legs were deeply grazed from ankle to thigh so I moved my attention to healing, mentally saying: "Body, heal yourself" and I visualizing the blood stopping and the healing already beginning. I focused all of my attention on those areas, seeing the healing, seeing the healing finished and leaving no scars. My energy was very powerful because I had no absolutely doubt that my body would obey me.

I promise you that the bleeding just stopped and I could see the skin calming down and the damaged areas sort of folding together as though not much had happened. There was no scarring!

EMERGENCY HEALING

Living in the Middle East in a new building of luxury apartments the telephone rang and the concierge said that my visitors were coming up in the lift. I was giving a coffee morning for people new to the Kingdom, people of several nationalities and I wanted everything to go smoothly. Running into the kitchen, in my haste to fill the kettle I spilled water on to the smooth floor tiles. The doorbell rang, and turning, my new shoes skidded on the water on the smooth tiled floor and I crash, head first against the hard wood of the door jamb!

Using the Silva Method was by now, second nature and pushing myself onto my knees I placed a hand on my temple and said, "Body heal yourself, body heal yourself, body heal yourself." I said that 3 times, the bell rang again; I stood up, walked to the door and entertained my guests with not a thought to what had happened in the kitchen.

I didn't even remember the incident until the next morning when, brushing my hair, I felt the interest bump of a bruise. Once again it was the power of my focus. I gave no thought to failure. This was an emergency and clear thinking in an emergency, is stock in trade for the Silva graduate.

INTUITION – USE IT OR LOSE IT!

Still in Saudi Arabia, one morning I had a sudden and distinct feeling that back in U.K., my son had had a car accident! I told my husband who said I should phone home and find out what the situation was – but I hesitated…

I was sure that he had had a car accident but my instinct/intuition, well developed and trusted by this time, said that he wasn't really hurt, and so I waited.

Three days later my son phoned to say: "Mother, I turned the car over three days ago but walked away with a few cuts and bruises."

Intuition used to be a natural instinct, trusted by people but when Mathew Hopkins was appointed Witch-Finder General, and had over 300 women murdered as witches in just two years (1644

– 1646) it got to a point where even farmers
were afraid to predict tomorrows weather!

And if you don't use it – you lose it!

DREAM CONTROL

I had a nightmare for many years, infrequent but always the same one. One of the mental techniques that Silva teaches is called Dream Control, and one night, not long after receiving my basic training, that nightmare started again. I was somehow outside of the scene, watching myself about to become a victim again. Then, just as the bad part was about to happen, and as though snapping out of a trance, I suddenly said: "Do your Silva!" My three fingers came together (the trigger) I took control, the nightmare stopped in its tracks – and it has never reoccurred! Here again, even in sleep, it was the strong focus of my thought and my total trust that I could handle this situation.

It is a fact that anyone or any organisation that wants to take control of your sovereignty; take away your free will to decide, is not working for your benefit. It usually comes down to either an obsessive desire to control another – or more and regular cash deposits in their bank!

DYSLEXIA

The Silva Method totally changed the dynamics of my life for the better. I could not document all the achievements, experiences and daily benefits that have helped and guided me over the years but ranking as one of the most remarkable, and critical to me as a writer, was my understanding of, and the overcoming of my inability to spell. This was totally due to my previously undiagnosed Dyslexia. Precious years were blighted by it and I was already into my forties when, using a Silva technique, I learned to spell virtually overnight! Changing my thinking (my concept of my reality) changed my life.

****

Aged nine, the girl stood in front of the class, exercise book held high for all to see the spelling mistakes scored through with red ink, slashing marks for an otherwise excellent composition. The teacher, believing that this (quite bright) student was being lazy, had encouraged the other children to laugh at her hopeless attempt at spelling. This was not to humiliate the girl but an effort to make her 'pay attention' and memorise the daily homework list of words. It didn't work and confidence was totally shattered. As the years passed there was always a dictionary at hand as every word over three letters was checked again and again before articles could be sold to newspapers or magazines because, 'I can't spell so I must be wrong.' I was that child and over thirty years later a sort of miracle happened.

Saudi Arabia. Midnight. It was the Holy month of Ramadan, and I woke because my husband was getting ready to leave for duty at the hospital. During this month, day is turned into night and human nature being what it is, people who have starved all day eat too much and too fast when the setting sun marks the end of the day. As a consequence, the hospital clinics are opened accordingly.

To put myself back to sleep I was meditating, mentally repeating words of a mantra when, in my mind's eye I saw the words being written – back to front! Mirror writing! Eyes wide, I sat up and then told my husband what had happened and he, kind and encouraging as ever, said I should take a pen and see if I could actually reproduce what I had visualised. I was reluctant, this was revolutionary thinking because over the years, proof reading my manuscripts, various people had asked if I could mirror write and, was I dyslexic, "Because there is a pattern here." I had always rejected this idea out of hand having been conditioned to think that dyslexia was an excuse. Embarrassing though it was, I would not pretend. I would never give myself an easy way out. I wouldn't risk another put-down from those who would ridicule me if did; take it on the chin, no excuses, I couldn't spell and that was a fact.

Now, trying to hold down the excitement, I got out of bed very slowly and, holding the picture in my mind's eye (Silva Method training), I continued to watch myself, doing something that I had assumed extraordinary and totally beyond my capabilities.

I didn't turn on the bedroom lamp but picking up pen and paper, went into the bathroom - and wrote as easily right to left as left to right, then upside down, then upside down and back to front! Then, with both hands, I wrote in opposite directions and upside down at the same time! I then held the paper up to the mirror. It was legible! How amazing was that?

The barrier was down! It wasn't an excuse. I really did have a diagnosable problem. I had been struggling valiantly with undiagnosed dyslexia for a lifetime and the knowledge was so freeing, so overwhelmingly marvellous, that I sobbed like a child! There wasn't a 'blank dumb section' in my brain that couldn't cope with spelling. There had to be a physical explanation.

Nystagmus: A slight weakness in holding focus, that flickered and rearranged the letters in a word, had been responsible for all those years of embarrassment, anxiety and misery. Now I was free! My belief in my limitations, gone!

I still have problems with long division, the numbers are too close together, but algebra was easy peasy. I've heard the same thing from other dyslexics. Somehow the layout and the patterns make sense to us.

Being able to spell freed my mind from many writing restrictions. If there wasn't a dictionary handy I would make up the text by using the words I could spell, often missing the impact of the point I was trying to make.

Accepting this fact that I was dyslexic wasn't enough. It wasn't an end but a beginning. I wanted to do something about it, understand how it was manifesting, and do something to correct it.

A couple of weeks earlier I had been in a coffee shop. The man next to me opened his newspaper and on the front page in huge headlines, I read:

'NIAGARA FALLS TO SELL OIL'

'They've struck oil at Niagara Falls!' I said in amazement to my husband who was sitting opposite – and the man with the newspaper looked at me as if I had gone mad. What the letters actually said were:

'NIGERIA FAILS TO SELL OIL

Not only were letters mixing up of their own accord but if they were also being physically moved as was the newspaper, or if I was driving and trying to follow sign post directions, the result was chaos. In that moment, I wanted the floor of the coffee shop to open up and swallow me but there was no way out, no covering up.

The actress and writer, Susan Hampshire, in her first enlightening and heartwarming book, "Every Letter Counts," echoed my stressful and ingenious ways of pretending that it had all been a 'silly mistake' and that I really knew the right answer.

I read with confidence from the age of four because I was somehow able to do what I later called block-reading, understanding the meaning of whole pages without actually reading every word. I was called a bookworm, devouring the contents but living in absolute dread of being asked to read aloud. Fortunately, and strangely, I had the ability to correctly interpret the mix of letters on the page. Unfortunately I wrote down the mixed-up words as I saw them! There was nothing wrong with my memory but I still occasionally put the 'T' in the middle of the word yacht, because that's how I see it. I used to joke that on a good day I could get seven letters in the name Jesus. On a bad day it could be eight. If in doubt, stick another letter in!

The point of this confession is that the undermining of my confidence as a child and my total acceptance that I couldn't spell (so I couldn't spell <u>anything)</u> was so ingrained that I couldn't think beyond it. No excuses. At spelling I was a duffer, yet it took only minutes to break the strangle hold of a lifetime. Confidence restored and accepting the challenge, I started to read more slowly, giving letters time to settle into the right place and I began to spell correctly, virtually overnight! AMAZING! WONDERFUL!

Yet it still concerns me and I do wonder just how many children have their potential stunted by adults, frustrated by the fact that the accepted ways of teaching are not showing the expected results, shifting the blame by resorting to angry and dismissive comments: "Oh, don't you understand? I've told you a dozen times. Pay attention. Listen to what I am saying. Oh, I give up with you." Taken up by classmates and repeated often enough, we probably say it to ourselves – subconsciously, thus producing a life-long and oh so unnecessary inhibition that can stretch across a lifetime – unless we teach them differently.

THE FUTURE

The world is in crisis. We are raping this earth of the bounty she once gave so freely. Mankind, manipulated by fear, continues conflict by endless ego posturing, delivering hate for hate and creating more things for which to be afraid. In my opinion, the only way out of the hell we are creating for ourselves is to re-examine and trust ourselves to the teachings of Jesus who said: 'Whatever I do, you can do and more'. He taught and demonstrated how, by simply acknowledging our own power, we can create Paradise on Earth (the words of Jose Silva), fuelled by the power of love. This book provides the guidelines – and so the rest is up to you.

Confucius said:
"Some people say they can do it, some people say they can't do it. They are both right because they will get what they ask for."

THE END

To find out more about June and her public appearances,
Google the following:

June Kidd Dyslexia

June Kidd Theosophical Society

June Kidd Science of Mind

TALKS

The Dismantling of the Parasite called Fear.

Crop Circles and Beyond.

The Universe Within Mirrors the Universe Without.

Learning to be Happy.

RECOMMENDED READING

THE SILVA METHOD HAND BOOK

Your key to success, fulfillment and personal growth, rapid
learning, sharper memory, improved health, happier
relationships and the attainment of new goals, accessing the
subconscious mind. ISBN 0 285 63541 7

To find out more, email:
better@silvamethod.uk.com
gostend@silvamethod.co.uk
Karin@silvamethod.uk.com

•••••

ET 101 BY DIANA LUPPI

We are universal travellers and co-creators of the life we live.
This book is for people with advanced thinking and an open
logical mind. ISBN 0-9626958-0-7

•••••

SCIENCE OF MIND BY ERNEST HOLMES

This is a philosophy, a faith and a way of life. It has a scientific approach to metaphysical subjects. In U.K., for Science of Mind, the Rev: Anya Turner, based in Bournemouth focuses on the integration of science and spiritual principles. After many years of personal growth, study into the powers of the mind and the psychology of successful living, Anya now teaches courses, conducts seminars, weekly gatherings and workshops, and also works with clients on a one-to-one basis for: Living a fulfilling life. revanya@scienceofmind.org ISBN 0-87477-921-9

•••••

COSMIC ORDERING BY JONATHAN CAINER

This is a joyous, encouraging, simple to understand, 'have-a-go,' book. ISBN 0-00-723644-1

•••••

BOOKS BY SUSAN HAMPSHIRE

Including *Every Letter Counts.* ISBN 0-593018869

•••••

ILLUSIONS BY RICHARD BACH

Illusions is mind expanding and fun to read. Bach is the author of *Jonathan Livingstone Seagull*, a book perfect for children who are asking questions. ISBN 0 330 25355 7

IN THE WORK PLACE

iCOACHING PLATFORM
(formerly known as JAYZOW)

Based on the Scandinavian policy of working with TRUST and CO-OPERATION in the work place, the iCOACHING PLATFORM, way is ground-breaking and cutting-edge. People using this support programme are happier at work, experience a better quality of life in general, are committed, enthusiastic and give more attention to developing new complimentary ideas. Get the best for, and from, your staff/teachers pupils/workforce, with the support of this new advanced staff coaching software.

JayZow software is totally different from anything on the market. So committed are we to delivering and expanding this new approach that we offer a no obligation, free, private demonstration. We just want to see your reaction!

To read actual feedback from satisfied and enthusiastic clients and to view your particular area of expertise, take a few moments to visit:

jayzowinspire.wordpress.com

Telephone: 07770885077

- Continual On-the-Job Personal Development
- Continually Raising Day-to-Day Standards
- Linked to Achieving Personal and Business Objectives

This unique all-in-one framework has comprehensive training included.